St Kilda

Text by David Quine

Photography by Colin Baxter

Colin Baxter Photography Ltd, Grantown-on-Spey, Scotland

The view from Mullach Mòr, Hirta's second highest hill, looks north over Glen Bay towards the Cambir and the silhouette of Soay, Britain's least visited isle.

Unique in thy structure
– as in the manner of thy sons
– thou sittest Queen of the Atlantic.

Lachlan MacLean, 1838

Pretty? No!
It is grand and awe inspiring
but not pretty!

Heathcote, 1900

St Kilda is the most isolated group of islands within the British Isles – although only a tiny dot on the map, the archipelago can compete with any as the finest nature reserve in western Europe. In 1987 its importance was recognised when it became Scotland's first 'World Heritage Site.' It is full of surprises – even the name St Kilda refers to no saint but comes from the old Norse 'skildir' (shields). From a distance the islands appear to rest on the water like the old Viking shields. An early cartographer in 1592 inserted a stop between S and K and so created S.Kilda. Hirta, the present name for the main island, comes from 'Hirtir' which appeared in an Icelandic Saga of a perilous voyage from Iceland to Ireland in the course of which a ship arrived at 'the islands that are called Hirtir.' Hirtir is old Norse for stags, since at closer

The vista from Boreray and Stac Lee towards the other islands of the archipelago forming the outer rim of the old volcano.

3

Fulmars cut through the air above Conachair's cliffs where 6,000 pairs nest below the shoulder of Uachdarachd. Four miles to the north, Stac an Armin, Stac Lee and Boreray provide the site of the largest gannetry in the world with over 60,000 pairs.

range the stacs, peaks and pinnacles rear up like the pointed antlers of a stag.

The magnificent view of the islands at the end of a crossing is always exciting. The memory fails to hold accurate images from year to year; the sheer stature of the cliffs of Oiseval, the rough saw-edged ridge of Dùn, the fang-like Stacs and the fantastic adjacent cliffs of Boreray are quite breathtaking.

The scenery reveals the geology. St Kilda emerged from a huge volcano 54-65 million years ago in the Tertiary Era, at the same time as the formation of Rum, Ardnamurchan, Arran, NE Ireland, and even the Faeroes, Iceland and Greenland. The archipelago was thrown up in an extensive period of plutonic activity between Hirta and Boreray. The rim of the volcano is defined by Soay, South and West Hirta, Dùn and Levenish, and curves round underwater to Boreray and the stacs. It is made up of dark rugged gabbro, the earliest rocks of St Kilda, which break up into great blocks like the Mistress Stone on Ruaival and the knobbly formation of the South and West coastline of Hirta, Boreray and the Stacs. The more rounded mountains of Oiseval and Conachair were the most recently formed, from a buff, light-coloured granophyre (fine grained granite), rich in quartz. Where this is exposed to the elements on the cliffs it tends to split into great slabs providing excellent ledges for nesting fulmars. Thick, dark bands of black dolerite, injected under great pressure, strike diagonally across these cliffs and help to form the caves at their foot. The smoothened stones on the storm beach of Village Bay reveal the dark blue-black dolerite and the buff granophyre.

Another very complex period of volcanic activity gave rise to other features such as the tunnel at Gob na h-Airde.

Over the centuries the continuous weathering, the onslaught of the sea and the rockfalls continue to form new sea caves and stacs. The mountains have become 'hills, but in reality they are only halves of hills, hills to the interior, but cliffs to the sea.' (Sands, 1878).

South over the ridge which rises steadily to Conachair's summit is the rounded form of Oiseval (Norse for East Fell). In the distance Levenish lies to the left and Dùn to the right.

The 50 miles of Atlantic Ocean separating St Kilda from the nearest land have always been a problem to anyone considering the crossing, but have rarely deterred the real adventurer. The fact is that Bronze Age Man accomplished it, reaching the islands and making his home on Hirta 3,000 years ago; among the rocks of Clash na Bearnaich he chipped away at the native dolerite manufacturing his stone tools. These were mostly hoe blades, a few were parts of a simple plough, others were for butchering animals and working with wood. Their food must have been

The slopes of Na h-Eagan lead down to Ruaival (Norse for Red Fell) and the Mistress Stone. A rough stretch of water separates this part of Hirta from the island of Dùn with its rugged summit ridge, home to over 40,000 pairs of puffins.

limpets, shellfish, fish, birds, seals, perhaps sheep supplemented with some crops and seaweed.

The Vikings arrived c900 and gave names to many of the islands and mountains: Soay – Sheep Island, Boreray – Fortified Island, Oiseval – East Fell, Ruaival – Red Fell. They also left two beautiful tortoise brooches but sadly these have now been lost. The St Kilda field mouse, which is twice the size of its close relatives, probably came over in a sack of hay with the Vikings whereas the little St Kilda wren, a slightly larger subspecies than its cousins, must have made its own way in spite of wind and waves. Other place names are Gaelic, originating from the settlers from Skye, and the Outer Hebrides – Harris and the Uists.

We are in the dark concerning the next phase of history until we get the earliest account of the islands by Hector Boece in 1527. He referred to the island of Hirta, the abundant sheep, the craggy nature of the rock, the single landing place and the sea – often terrible and rough. He mentioned the June visit of a priest who came to baptize infants, say masses and receive tithes of all their commodities and then returned home.

Dean Monro in 1549 gave a fuller account mentioning the ownership of MacLeod of Harris, the large sheep, good grass and corn. He said the people were unlearned. The steward made his midsummer visit and collected dues paid in dried wildfowl, mutton and seals.

In 1697 Martin Martin from Skye visited the islands and found a population of 180. His book, a real classic, describes in detail the islands, the people (down to their beards), and the natural history, including an eyewitness account of the great auk.

The population was devastated by a smallpox outbreak in 1727. A man from St Kilda who was visiting Harris, caught the disease and died. The next year one of his friends carried his clothes back to Hirta and it is thought that these were the source of the infection which eventually caused 94 deaths, and left only four adults and 26 children from 21 families. Among the survivors were three men and eight boys who had been marooned on Stac an Armin from October until the following June.

Before the disease we know only the names of MacDonalds, Morrisons and Gilliverarys as they formed the core of the next generation. St Kilda was repopulated with families from Harris –

Part of the Village Street showing the arc of 1860 cottages including one of several repaired by the National Trust for Scotland Work Parties.

The mist can spill down at any time, often in the cool of the evening, giving an atmospheric feel to the deserted Village Street, and emphasising the contrasting shapes of the early rounded 1830's black-houses and the angular 1860 cottages.

the Fergusons and Morrisons; from Skye – the Gillies, MacCrimmons, MacKinnons, MacLeods (possibly from Harris) and the MacDonalds; from North Uist – the MacQueens.

Thomas Dyke Acland from Devon visited St Kilda in 1812 and painted the first known watercolours of the islands and the village. He returned in 1834 to find a new Kirk and Manse already built, but feeling concerned for the natives, he left £20 with the Minister, the Rev Neil MacKenzie, to stimulate the demolition of their old hovels and the building of new houses. This began soon after his visit, and many of these remain today, becoming byres when the sixteen '1860 cottages' were built after a dreadful October storm.

When the Minister left in 1844 the people seemed unsettled and leaderless. In 1852 thirty-six of the inhabitants accepted the offer of the Highlands and Islands Emigration Society to start a new life in Australia. This was a disaster in two ways – fewer than half survived the dreadful voyage and their departure crippled the close-knit community. The population never recovered. This was partly due to the deaths of so many healthy babies who succumbed to infantile tetanus, known as 'eight day sickness'.

During the First World War a small naval detachment lived on

St Kilda and spread unrest among the young men by recommending an easier way of life in Glasgow. At the end of the war many left, twelve in one group, which was a terrible blow to the manpower of the island. The last years of the 1920s were very hard with few fit men to work with the boats and cultivate the agricultural plots. In 1926 four of the key men died in one week in an influenza outbreak.

The severe and prolonged winter of 1929-30 was devastating, with no mainland contact for several months, leaving some families at near starvation level. Then two of the young people died, finally cracking the spirit of the St Kildans. The population had dropped to 36 souls and the people were, on the whole, ready to leave for an uncertain future. Cattle and sheep left on the *SS Hebrides* for Tiree, and the *SS Dunara Castle* for the markets in Oban together with the bulk of their luggage and furniture. On Friday 29th August 1930, *HMS Harebell* took the inhabitants from their island home, the only world they knew. Most of them disembarked at Lochaline, Morvern, on the west of mainland Scotland, where they found accommodation in the village, while others went to nearby Larachbeg, Achabeg, Savaroy and Ardness. The Fergusons and the Minister went on to Oban. All were to begin a very different way of life – many were employed in forestry although they had never seen a tree in their lives – many suffered from TB and only survived a few years.

The islands were sold by Sir Reginald MacLeod to the 5th

The silvery sea between Hirta and Boreray disguises the dangers experienced by the St Kildans who had a great fear and respect for its unpredictable nature. Soay and the Cambir are just distinguishable in the distance.

9

Boat-shaped settings, dating from 1850 BC, can be found on An Lag, the valley north of the Village, up to the Gap. The stones are buried to half their depth and each structure is longer than it is wide, with most coming to a point at both ends. Their purpose is still uncertain.

Marquis of Bute who ran St Kilda as a bird reserve. Neil Gillies, a St Kildan, was employed as his chief warden, staying from May until August between 1931 and 1939 when the war broke out. At one time the owner had to put nine watchmen on the island to stop foreign trawler men from raiding the houses for their contents. Over 100 sheep of mixed age and sex were transferred from the island of Soay to Hirta's now vacant pastures where they have been studied continuously with very little interference from man.

The islands were bequeathed in 1956 to the National Trust for Scotland who eventually accepted the gift the following year having been anxious about the care and protection of such a distant outpost. Around this time, the RAF built a services camp which remains a blot on the landscape, but is essential for the Ministry of Defence in their support of the civilian rocket tracking team.

Annual NTS work parties were established to conserve the buildings and monitor the wildlife, and research was carried out on seabird numbers, vegetation and sheep. Fascinating archaeological projects have resulted in the discovery of Bronze Age tool quarries on the eastern slope of Clash-na-Bearnaich.

In 1987 St Kilda became a World Heritage Site, and detailed research has been carried out on the marine environment including shore and diving surveys using the latest remote operated vessel and sonar work on the seabed. The islands have also been designated a Special Area of Conservation for Scottish Natural Heritage.

The amphitheatre of Village Bay from the massive rocks on the summit of Dùn.
On the left is Mullach Bi (355m, 1165ft) with the boulder field of Carn Mòr below. The tall radio mast is visible on
Mullach Mòr with the ridge rising to the top of Conachair – the highest point of the archipelago (425m, 1394ft).

The village nestled comfortably in the hollow of the hills, as if waiting the return of its vanished people. I felt deeply moved on scanning the ruins of their ocean solitude. The silence, I thought was not of the moment but of the ages.

John Morton Boyd on his first visit to St Kilda in 1952

The first impression of one visitor as he landed on Hirta was that the St Kildans must have suffered from a consuming obsession – to spend their time and energy using up all the surrounding stone to erect buildings – houses, walls, store-houses, gravestones, wells and a saw-pit. All the buildings on St Kilda are constructed of stone and there is no shortage of it – huge quantities can be found at the edge of the village below Conachair, the highest 'hill'. Within and below the screes of Clash na Bearnaich there are some of the earliest cellular and ancient structures. But practically the whole evolutionary span of the buildings can be traced within the Village and just outside the Head Dyke.

The Souterrain or earth-house was an early tunnel-shaped building set wholly underground with two annexes. It was possibly used for storage or as a hiding place when unknown piratical boats appeared in the bay.

Early dwellings included small circular houses like green mounds, with stone walls 2m thick and spaces for beds and

Village Bay, the Kyle of Dùn and Ruaival form a background to sheep enclosures on An Lag which can also be seen above the Village and its Head Dyke (opposite).

The Village nestles in the sweep of Village Bay, bounded by Oiseval on the left with Dùn and Ruaival to the right. The Kyle of Dùn, which separates the rugged breakwater of Dùn from Hirta, is narrow with fierce tide-races, and rarely navigable, but St Kildans negotiated it at low tide by jumping from rock to rock.

stores. The corbelled roofs were completely covered by turf, some having one or more beehive annexes. There were no tables or chairs, just wooden stools and stones. The taller 'Medieval House' with beehive annexe had its walls visible. These houses formed the village when Henry Brougham visited in 1799. He landed in Glen Bay, walked over the ridge of Am Blaid and looking down he saw,

'several green tufts of grassy sod, upon heaps of loose stones – these we at last discovered to be the houses, 26 in number...This is the town or city of St Kilda. It contains 100 inhabitants; the rest of the island is only browsed by some sheep, horses and cows. The view of this village is unique.'

Black-houses were erected after the visit of Sir Thomas Dyke Acland in 1834 and within a few years a whole settlement grew up. Black-houses were built with a double wall, the wooden roof resting on the inner one, covered by flattened barley thatch held down by ropes and stones. Some had a window, some a granny flat; in winter the cow was kept in one half, the family in the other. Some basic pieces of furniture were also provided, beds were built into the wall, and irrespective of the number of occupants there were never more than two bed chambers – people disappeared in holes in the wall like a puffin retiring to its burrow.

The next stage in the development of the Village came in 1860 when a severe October gale took the roofs off some of the black-houses. The owner sent out his own stonemason from Skye – so began the building of 16 rectangular-shaped cottages. The black-houses became byres for the cattle and storage for birds, grain, fish and potatoes.

From 1834 onwards other buildings were erected for special functions – a saw-pit to use any logs washed up on the shore, walls and cupolas constructed over the wells, a corn drying kiln, a mill, gardens and enclosures (planticrubs) for growing a few vegetables. Cleitean, a St Kildan invention of small, turf-roofed, storage and drying buildings were constructed, some 1,260 on Hirta alone. The turf absorbed the rain, and the wind whistled through the walls desiccating any contents. Those in the Village were primarily for storing and drying hay, but also fish, birds,

The roofless houses in the Village Street paint a poignant picture of life in the past. The 1860 cottages dominate, while the older 1830's houses became byres for the cattle and covered space for the threshing of crops and the storage of grain, fulmars, potatoes and fish.

The 1860 cottages in the Village at the time of this photograph (1886) still had their original zinc roofs. As someone observed, 'when it rained outside, it also rained inside!' These were later replaced by felt and tar held down with wooden battens. The view shows the agricultural plots in use and the glebe enclosure around the Kirk and the manse; the feather store lies beyond.

peat and turf. A further 170 are found on the other islands and stacs (40 on Soay, 50 on Boreray, 80 on Stac an Armin). The Head Dyke, enclosing the Village and agricultural plots, was built using massive blocks of stone to keep the sheep and cattle out during the spring and summer growth.

On St Kilda five buildings had slated roofs – the Factor's House, built in the 1860s, for the use of the Factor when he came to collect the rent, and the Kirk, Manse, feather-store and schoolroom. School was held in the Factor's House from 1884 but in 1898 masons and carpenters arrived from Dunvegan to build the new schoolroom. Lessons were often interrupted or never started as the school log records – 'No school today...heavy snow, every house washing tweed; no school for three weeks – influenza, people gathering birds' eggs, Mrs MacKinnon's baby is sick; no school for a week – all engaged in killing and salting the fulmar, children bringing peats from the hill for the school fire, great storm raging; church and school being cleaned for a marriage.'

Three churches were recorded at the end of the 17th century, but by 1799 the buildings had fallen into decay and services were being held in the Parson's house. Brougham describes the situation, 'A more wretched hovel never sheltered beast from the storm than this' and describes the Sunday Service, 'This being Sunday...the whole congregation was assembled in the Parson's kitchen, men, women and children. The Parson himself was seated upon a large bag of feathers with a barrel of oil before him by way of reading desk.' (Brougham, 1799).

In the 1820s the Rev Dr John MacDonald, the Apostle of the North, having seen the needs of the people of St Kilda for himself, collected money for the building of a new Kirk, which was ready in 1830 for the arrival of the Rev Neil MacKenzie who masterminded the new planned settlement. Connel (1887) reminds us that time was not important, 'The morning service began at 11am – not according to Greenwich, but according to MacKay.' It was in the Kirk that their Christian Faith was nurtured, sustaining them and strengthening them in times of hardship and tragedy. In their own homes on a daily basis, first place was given to family worship which included Bible reading and prayer. This also took place when they were out in the boat fishing and even on the cliffs of Boreray as they were collecting gannets – work would stop for worship. The people were resilient, adaptive, caring and sharing.

The schoolchildren in their 'Sunday best' in 1886 with their teacher, George Murray, who came for one year and kept a fascinating detailed diary of the yearly cycle and crises of the inhabitants.

November – this is the deadest month of the year. There is a pleasure in seeing anything move in this more than solitary place. Our minds seem to be revived by seeing a few wildfowl such as swans, geese, woodcocks and snipes, though most of them pay us but a short visit on their way to more hospitable climes.

Rev Neil MacKenzie, St Kilda, 1830-44

Winter was always a difficult time in 'the windiest place in Britain' with short days and long nights, and only a poor flickering light from burning fulmar oil. Schoolmaster Ross (1889) dreaded the thought of winter on St Kilda where 'the medicine chest contained little but fulmar oil, castor oil, mustard and whisky!' The cattle were moved into the black-houses and the weaker sheep into available buildings, but they all had to be fed. After a long winter peat would run out. The best peats were dug from Gleann Mòr and dried out in cleitean on the ridge near the summit of Mullach Bi. Occasionally long lines of natives carrying their bags could be seen against the snow as they descended the white hills.

The men and women were always busy, the women carding and spinning the wool, and later waulking the tweed. The men were weavers, tailors and cobblers in winter and during the rest

Turbulent waters churn through the Kyle of Dùn and into the many caves under the western face of Dùn. The rugged ridges of Dùn are formed from the primitive dark and resistant gabbro rocks which give the characteristic stark corrugated contours.

The banner-cloud clings onto Boreray's buttresses and summit (379m, 1243ft) and round the fingers of Clagan na Rùsgachan (236m, 774ft), Skull Rock of the Fleeces (opposite).

The gannet was known to the St Kildans as 'Suliere' – the sharp-eyed. Spotting herring and mackerel from 30m above they dive in spectacular fashion, plummeting under the surface of the water. They are mature after six years and nest on Boreray and the neighbouring stacs, laying a single egg in early May. Incubation is six weeks and the young are deserted after 11 weeks. St Kildans collected adults, eggs and young at different times of the year.

of the year, crofters, cragsmen and fishermen.

With the arrival of spring, agricultural plots had to be dug over and manured, potatoes planted and lambs cared for. Everyone longed for the lengthening days and the appearance of migrating birds which would give a change in diet from salted fulmar, mutton and dried fish.

George Murray, the schoolmaster (1886-7) recorded in his diary, 'On Thursday April 7th I went with the men to Boreray to kill gannets through the night…When the night began to fall seven went on land and five remained in the boat to cruise round the island to pick up the birds when thrown over the rocks…Being a full moon it was much too clear for making what they call 'good work'. I did not complain of the clearness at all as I could, in places where no cat could get, see where I was going. It is very dangerous work on a dark night. After working for an hour or two we rested and had Family Worship. The scene to me was very impressive. The three of us sat down on the bare rocks with ropes about our middle, the cloudless sky our canopy, the moon our lamp, and the ocean still and quiet far below, and offered praise and prayer to Him who was able to preserve us in such dangerous work.'

During the summer, cows were kept at the Gleann Mòr and milked there by the women who then had to carry the milk back; lambs had to be collected, identified and earmarked and the sheep rounded up to be sheared – a terrific task on Hirta, but even more difficult on Boreray where the men would stay for a week or so. Girls would spend a week on Soay and another week on Boreray to catch puffins and pluck them for the feather export. Men would take their dogs with them at night to go to the boulder field of Carn Mòr just below Mullach Bi to catch Manx shearwaters as they left their burrows or returned from their fishing trips. In the evenings in good weather the men would lay the long lines, stay the night in their boat in one of the caves in Boreray and lift the lines in the morning. But St Kildans and the ocean did not get on well together – they had good reason to respect and fear the sea.

Autumn was a very busy time on St Kilda. Ropes were tested, the most precious article they possessed, before the Fulmar Harvest began around August 12 and continued for eight days. This involved descending the cliffs on ropes to secure the young fulmars, and bringing them back to the Village to be plucked and

Looking across Glen Bay towards Boreray, the waters rushing through the tunnel under Gob na h-Airde are a favourite place for grey seals to play and haul out on the rocks for rest.

The young fulmar was essential to the welfare of the St Kildans, their oil for lamps and medicine, their flesh salted and stored in barrels for winter food. Men descended the precipitous cliffs on ropes working in pairs along the narrow fulmar ledges, collecting about 100 birds for each person to last until the spring.

salted for winter food. One visitor reported, 'The air is full of feathered animals, the sea is covered with them, the houses are ornamented by them, the ground is speckled with them like a flowery meadow in May. The town is paved with feathers, the very dung-hills are made of feathers...the inhabitants look as if they have been tarred and feathered, for their hair is full of feathers and their clothes are covered with feathers. The women look like feathered Mercuries, for their shoes are made of gannets' skin; everything smells of feathers, and the smell pursued us all over the islands – for the captain had concealed a sackful in the cabin.' (MacCulloch J. 1819).

The Gannet Harvest was later in September or October and involved landing on Boreray for a week and daily visits to Stac Lee and Stac an Armin. They were so skilled on the cliffs that Seton (1878) commented, 'to anyone who has witnessed a St Kilda cragsman, the most startling feats of Léotard or Blondin appear utterly insignificant.' Then there was the haymaking which went on week after week, the hay being stored and dried in cleitean in the village.

On such an isolated archipelago as St Kilda, it was necessary for the men to communicate regularly with each other. Most mornings they would meet outside the post office or nearby house to discuss and plan the activities of the day. Sometimes it was midday before decisions were made but the discussions united the community and kept people informed as to everyone's whereabouts. Sands, who was marooned on St Kilda in 1876, commented, 'I called this assembly the Parliament, and with a laugh they adopted the name. When the subject is exciting the members talk with loud voices all at one time. Some of the men may be seen reclining on the top of the wall of an old hut, others leaning against it, hands in their pockets and their beards in the air, bawling at full pitch of their powerful voices. Shall we go to catch solan geese, or ling, or mend the boat or hunt sheep, are examples of the subjects that occupy the house.'

Another writer commented, 'Neighbouring Boreray was the limit of their foreign policy: even then, that policy was concerned solely with sheep, seabirds and their eggs.' (MacGregor A. A. 1969). In work everyone followed his neighbour. If one put a new thatch on his barn, a man was seen on top of every barn in the village.

Alice MacLachlan, the wife of the missionary, lived on St Kilda for three years, 1906-9, and kept a detailed diary. A few brief

THE ST KILDA PARLIAMENT. 6198 J G.W.W.

The St Kilda Parliament met daily to plan their affairs. The nearest man on the right is Donald Ferguson, the Ground Officer or senior man on the island. The small man, third from the left, is Donald MacDonald who, with two others, was chosen to represent the islanders before the Napier Commission in 1883. This six-man Royal Commission was instructed to enquire into 'The condition of the crofters and cottars in the Highlands and Islands of Scotland'.

Rising 166m (545ft) above sea level, the fang-like pinnacle Stac Lee also plunges 46m (150ft) vertically below the surface where the sea has gouged out a long sloping cave.

Stac Lee and Stac an Armin (opposite), as viewed from the cliffs of Hirta.

extracts catch the flavour of life on the islands.

'1906: September – opened school today (4th), cutting and raking hay – putting it into cleits; all the whalers away (14th); cut up and salted sheep, ordered four (15th).

October – people spinning and carding, salting sheep, wishing for more wind to dry the hay in the cleits, cutting hay on Conachair (cliffs), making cheese and butter.

1907: January – get ready for children's tea at three o'clock. Snow again – up the village to see the invalids. Baby very poorly. Fearful night, awful wind.

February – men went today to Soay (1st); trawler, Knowsie from Aberdeen, brings mail and takes our orders (12th); Knowsie brought back all we ordered (18th).

March – four trawlers working at Boreray (4th); Knowsie back bringing cheese, flour, jam, syrup, cream of tartar and sweets (7th); Capt of Knowsie brought out potatoes, toffee, sugar, almonds and blacking. Brought me a bag of oranges and apples, ginger beer and kippers from Stornoway.

April – Terrible gale today – in came the Knowsie, but it was impossible for our boats to venture. The Knowsie stayed all day till evening when she sailed out in a perfect hurricane, the waves washing her from end to end and almost turning her over.

May – First whaling boat in (3rd); men to Boreray, home with lambs, puffins and some gannets' eggs (6th); men to Boreray and Stac Lee for gannets' eggs (11th); three drifters in for herring (15th); people started cutting peat today (27th); whale in the Bay.'

Above us were the soaring crags, now looking so much more perpendicular, more chillingly out-swept than they had appeared from the boat, and above, thousands of wheeling gannets.

John Morton Boyd as he prepares to climb Stac Lee

'The west coast of Scotland has long been famous for possessing one of the richest seabird communities in the world.' (Bourne and Harris 1979). Here the Gulf Stream mixes with the colder waters of the Atlantic, supplying and circulating vital nutrients for the plant and animal plankton. These in turn provide food for the sand eels and fish; particularly important are the herring and mackerel which form the main food for the huge seabird colonies. The islands provide an ideal breeding base with isolated stacs, cliffs, ledges and burrows meeting the different preferences of the species. The different seabirds travel varying distances from the colonies to reach their food, gannets 150km, Manx shearwaters 100km and puffins up to 50km at times.

On the sloping roof of Stac Lee, 5,000 pairs of gannets sit cheek by jowl.

The awe-inspiring Stac an Armin and Boreray from the sea (opposite). At 191m, 627ft, Stac an Armin is the highest sea stac in Britain and the nesting site for 12,000 pairs of gannets.

The puffin, known to the St Kildans as 'Buigire' – the damp fellow, since he arrives on the nesting cliffs in damp weather early in April.

The isolation of St Kilda with 80km (50 miles) of Atlantic Ocean between the archipelago and the nearest sizeable land mass has severely limited the number of plants, animals and people reaching the islands and getting a foothold. For seabirds this has not been a problem. Although only 28 species of birds breed regularly, over one million birds frequent the islands during the summer. Gannets, 60,000 pairs, nest on the more isolated outposts of Boreray, Stac Lee and Stac an Armin; puffins, a quarter of the British population, nest in burrows or crevices in the boulders on all the islands and rocks except Stac Lee; guillemots, razorbills and fulmars nest on ledges in huge numbers. Manx shearwaters, storm and Leach's petrels (one of only five known breeding sites in Europe) are in great numbers. There are few predators, no resident eagles or owls, usually two pairs of peregrine falcons breed, and most damage is done by the great skuas and the great black-backed gulls, together with hooded crows and ravens. This makes St Kilda the most important seabird colony in western Europe.

Without a 'land-bridge' in recent geological history, amphibians and reptiles have not colonized the islands, and no frogs, toads, newts, snakes or lizards have been recorded. Few mammals have established themselves, only those that could swim, like grey seals, and those brought in by boat whether intentionally – Soay and blackface sheep (cows and horses in the past) – or inadvertently – St Kilda field mouse and the now extinct St Kilda house mouse.

Since the Quaternary Ice Sheet did not reach the group, the islands form a reservoir for pre-glacial plants. The dominant vegetation is maritime grassland which has been modified by a number of factors – high winds clip the heather to the equivalent of that growing around 800m on the mainland; selective grazing by the sheep has favoured the growth of heather and bracken; a lack of burning has enabled bilberry and the great woodrush to spread unhindered, particularly on the higher summits. Salt spray adversely affects many species causing considerable damage and limiting them to those adapted to survive such conditions. Seabird guano is another dominating factor on the cliff ledges where common sorrel is one of the few plants which can tolerate the high nitrogen content. As a considerable part of the land surface is between 200 and 425m above sea level this reduces the plant growth rate considerably. Cool summers also reduce the growth rate and badly affected crops.

A number of arctic-alpines have managed to establish themselves. St Kildans used other plants – lichens for dyeing, tormentil for tanning and barley stalks for thatch. Scurvy-grass, laver (seaweed), silverweed, common dock

Shafts of light illuminate the summit slopes of Conachair with Soay behind.

Eerie light sets off the savage silhouette of Dùn with its dramatic natural arch and rock pinnacles.

and carragheen were all used to supplement their diet.

Today, St Kilda still casts its spell and attracts people with a wide variety of interests. There are those wishing to explore the spectacular scenery and to experience such a wild and remote place. Others give their time, energy and skills for two weeks on work parties organised by the National Trust for Scotland. They carry out necessary practical maintenance work – painting, drainage, re-felting the cottage roofs, repairing collapsed walls and re-turfing cleits.

Skin-divers, captivated by the clarity of the water, claim it to be as beautiful and fascinating under water as above; they swim with seals and puffins in the huge cathedral-like caves off Boreray and admire delicate fan worms, colourful sea slugs and starfish, great walls of different species and hues of sea anemones. Others are involved in research into seabird numbers and their diets, the vegetation and Soay sheep; special weeks are set aside for archaeology and historians can follow their interests and wonder at the adaptability of man to survive in such a hostile environment. Each can pursue his interests in the context of the finest seabird colonies in western Europe.

This magnificent archipelago must be protected at all costs.

St Kilda

0 — 1 km

0 — 1 mile

Inset — overview map

0 — 5 km

0 — 2 miles

Boreray

Soay

Hirta

Dùn

Levenish

Boreray (inset)

Stac an Armin 191m
Am Biran
Bothy
Rubha Bhriste
Gearr-geo
An t-Sàil
Udraclete
Geo na Tarnanach
Mullach an Eilein
Geo Shunadail
379m
Sunadal
Boreray
Mullach an Tuamail
Creagan na Rubhaig Bana
Taigh Stallar
236m
Clesgor
Bothies
Creagan Fharspeig
Geo an Fheanchdaire
149m
Bothy 166m
Geo na Lee
Cleitein McPhaidein
Coinneag
94m
Geo an Aratch
Geo na Leachan Màire
Rubha Bhrengeadail
Stac Lee
Geo Sgarbhstac
Gob Scapanish
Sgarbhstac

The Boreray island group lies 6.1 kms (3.8 miles) N. East of Leac Mhìn Stac

Soay

Am Plàsdair
Poll Adinet
Creagan
Geo Rubha
Cave
308m
The Altar
Stac Soay
Tobar Ruadh
373m
Glamasgeo
Cnoc Glas
Mol Shoay
339m
Stac Biorach
Taigh Dugan
Gob a' Ghaill
Gob na h-Airde
Pursan a' Chaim
179m
Stac Dona
Soay
144m
Geo Phursan
Gob Phursan

Hirta

Geo Chaluim Mhic Mhuirich
The Cambir
211m
Geo Sgeir Chàise
Gob na h-Airde
Geo na h-Airde
Geo Oscar
Geo an t-Saoil
Na Cleitean
Mol Càrn na Liana
Loch a'Ghlinne or Glen Bay
Tunnel
Bradastac
Min Stac
Geo Chirubi
Geo nan Plaidean
Leac Mhìn Stac
Beul na Geo
Geo nan Ron
Baghan
Geo Bhradastac
Geo na Stacan
Mullach Mòr
Sgeir Dhomhnaill
272m
Geo na Laisealaich
Amazon's House
72m
Conachair
425m
Mol Ghiasgar
Stac a' Langa
355m
Radar Station
The Gap
Geo a' Bhroige
Am Broig
Geo an Eige
163m
Gleann Mòr
Leathad a' Ghlinne
Glacan Chonachair
Rubha Ghill
Calum Mòr's House
Lag Bho'n Tuath
121m
Geo na Muir-bhuaile (Bream)
Mullach Geal
Medieval House
Kiln
Sgeir nan Sgarbh
Mullach Bì
355m
Claigeann an Taigh Faire
The Village
Saw Pit
Oiseval
289m
Geo nan Sgarbh
Carn Mòr
289m
Am Blaid
Well
Pier
22m
Rubha Uisge
Sgeir Mhòr
Claigeann Mòr
282m
39m
Hirta
Geo na Eireanach
Gob Chathaill
Lover's Stone
Mullach Sgar
Clash na Bearnaich
218m
Point of Coll or Rubha Challa
Geo Creag an Arpaid
Leathaid a Sgithoil Chaoil
Mast
26m
Geo Brababy
Geo na Ba Glaise
Làimhrig nan Gall
Rubha Mhuirich
178m
Tobar na Gille
St. Brianan's Chapel
Uamh Cailleach Bheag Ruaival
An Torc
Geo Chile Brianan
Ruaival
Geo Leibli
135m
29m
Giasgeir
Mistress Stone
Geo Gharran Buidhe
Sgeir Mhòr
Altar
Sellis Geo
Geo na Ruideig
A' Bhi 113m
Tunnel
Bioda Mòr
176m
Na Bodhan
Dùn
Geo Gluasgeig
24m
Tunnel
Na Sgarain
A' Chuilc
Gob an Dùin
Sgeir Cùl an Rubha
Gob na Muce
Giumachsgor
Hamalan

Levenish (inset)

Na Bodhan
56m
Levenish

Levenish lies 2.8 kms (1.75 miles) E.N.East of Gob an Dùin

Location inset

Flannan Isles
Lewis
St Kilda
Harris
North Uist
Benbecula
Skye
South Uist
Barra
Rum

0 — 30 km
0 — 20 ml

Legend

● Place of interest
=== Surfaced road
≈ Village "street"
◇ Building
· Cleitein
⌇ Stone enclosure
— Dyke
⊙ Well
▓ Contour(30 metres)/cliff
≈ River/stream
░ Sandy beach

© Wendy Price Cartographic Services, Inverness, 2002.
Map based on the 1928 Ordnance Survey map with additions from aerial photography kindly supplied by Photoair through Scottish Natural Heritage. Whilst every care has been taken to ensure that the map is correct, it should not be used in a situation where a high degree of detail is required.